Ancient Greece for Kids

A Captivating Guide to Greek History, from the Mycenean Civilization and the Trojan War through the Golden Age of Pericles to the Hellenistic Era and Roman Conquests

Table of Contents

INTRODUCTION

Come dive into the world of the Ancient Greeks! Both parents and children will enjoy learning what made Ancient Greece such an amazing civilization and seeing why the modern world owes them so much. From their myths and culture to their wars and ultimate defeat by the Romans, this book covers it all.

For example, did you know that Greeks were some of the first people to figure out a way to write down their language? Reading is so common today; it's easy to take for granted that people have always done it. The Greeks wrote about their good and bad leaders, told fantastic stories about their gods and goddesses, and sometimes did both at the same time. Historians have a tricky job separating fact from fiction in Ancient Greece, but at least they are always entertained.

https://commons.wikimedia.org/wiki/
File:Helene_Paris_Louvre_K6.jpg

This book also gets readers up-close-and-personal with the first Olympic Athletes, the Spartan King Leonides and Alexander the Great. Get ready to hop into your time machine and see how civilization began and thrived in this part of the world!

The **Mycenaeans** were the first **civilization** from **Greece,** and they lasted from about 1600 BCE until 1100 BCE. Today, Greece is made up of a **peninsula** and several islands in southeastern Europe. But what does it mean to be "from somewhere"? After all, if you go back far enough, almost everyone comes from somewhere else. The Mycenaeans were probably a mixture of people who came from the area north of the Black Sea and the **Minoan** civilization from the island of **Crete**.

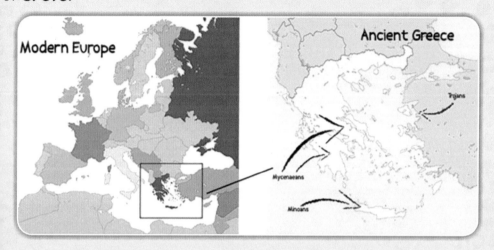

A big reason that historians only *probably* know this is because they haven't figured out how to read the Minoan language. Historians have had to look at similarities in things like art, buildings, and alphabets to make good guesses about the Minoan-Mycenaean connection. Historians can also learn a lot through **oral history**, which is the name for the stories people tell each other instead of writing them down. Sometimes they change a little bit as one person tells the next person, like a game of telephone that lasts for hundreds of years!

One story from Mycenaean oral history is about **King Minos** of Crete, which is where the term "Minoan" comes from. King Minos was a son of the Greek god **Zeus** and a mortal woman named **Europa**. After their son was killed in a war with the Mycenaean **city-state** of **Athens**, Minos demanded that Athens send seven boys and seven girls each year to be devoured by his beast called the **Minotaur**. The Minotaur had the body of a giant human and the head of a bull, and it lived beneath Minos' palace in a complicated maze called a **labyrinth**. This ritual lasted until a hero named **Theseus** volunteered to go and end the slaughter, and he fought and killed the Minotaur in a bloody battle. Theseus escaped the labyrinth with the help of Minos' daughter **Ariadne**, and the two of them sailed back to Athens together.

https://commons.
wikimedia.org
/wiki/File:Minotaur.
jpg#file

https://flyclipart.com/jigsaw-
puzzles-hedge-maze-labyrinth-
labyrinth-clipart-913499

So, what does this story tell us? Well, it lets us know that the Minoans and Mycenaeans were **rivals**, meaning that they were about equally powerful and often fought one another. It also tells us that they probably made peace through the marriage of important people. After all, Ariadne was a Minoan princess, and Theseus was a Mycenaean prince. At least in the story, anyway. But stories usually have some truth in them, even wild ones about a teenager fighting a murderous bull-monster in the middle of a crazy king's special maze. Because it's oral history, the details are sometimes different depending on who you hear it from. In some versions, Theseus uses a sword to defeat the Minotaur, but he can do it with just his bare hands in others. No matter what, though, Theseus always beats the Minotaur and saves Greek children from the evil King Minos.

What made the Mycenaean culture flourish and survive for so long? They lasted for about 500 years, which is more than twice as long as the United States has been a country! One of the biggest reasons was that Mycenae, their main

city-state, was a huge fortress. For hundreds of years, their people were able to live behind its walls, safe from their enemies. When people are safe, they can worry about more than just survival.

This usually leads to a **golden age** for civilizations, and it's when things like art, music, sports, games, and all the fun things in life are common. After all, would you be able to enjoy a day at the beach if there were a bunch of people fighting over it? Come to think of it, fighting on a beach is something that the Mycenaeans famously did near the end of their golden age. They fought for *ten long years* on the shores by another great, rival city-state called **Troy**.

Across the **Aegean Sea**, in what is now the country of Turkey, was a city-state called **Troy**. The people who lived in Troy were called **Trojans**, and the story of the Trojan War begins when their two princes paid a royal visit to **King Menelaus** of **Sparta**. The older prince, **Hector**, was known as the greatest warrior in all of Troy. But it was the younger prince, **Paris**, who started all the trouble when he saw the king's beautiful wife, **Queen Helen**. Depending on which version you hear, Paris and Helen either fell in love and ran away together, or she was kidnapped by the young prince and taken back to Troy. Either way, **King Agamemnon** of Mycenae used the incident to convince Menelaus to declare war against Troy sometime around 1200 BCE.

When Hector and Paris returned to Troy with Helen, their dad (**King Priam**) knew that there would be trouble coming behind them. Agamemnon and Menelaus soon arrived at their shore with over 1,000 ships, and the Trojan War had begun! Unfortunately for the Greeks, Troy's walls were too tall, too strong, and too well guarded for them to get inside the city. Fortunately for the Greeks, they had a powerful warrior and half-god named **Achilles**. In the Greeks' story, Achilles was dipped into the magical **River Styx** by his mother, who was holding him upside down by his foot. The river's magic made him almost invincible, except for the heel his mother held onto him by.

https://upload.wikimedia.org/wikipedia/en/5/58/Triumph_
of_Achilles_in_Corfu_Achilleion.jpg

After years of fighting the Trojans with no clear victory, Achilles grew bored and told Agamemnon that he was leaving. His best friend, **Patroclus**, was worried that the other Greeks would see him go - and then give up. He took Achilles' armor and led the Greek army into their next battle so they would believe he was still with them. When Prince Hector saw Patroclus in the armor, he mistook him for the real Achilles. Hector fought and killed Patroclus, discovering - only afterward - that it was not the great Greek hero. Enraged, Achilles returned to challenge Hector to one-on-one combat. Achilles proved to be the stronger warrior, killing Hector outside the gates of Troy.

Still, Troy did not surrender, and the Greeks could not get inside the walls for ten years. That's when another Greek leader named **Odysseus** had a clever idea. Following his plan, the Greek army sailed away during the night so that the Trojans would believe they had finally given up and gone home. They left a giant wooden horse on the beach as a gift to the Trojans to honor their victory. However, inside of the wooden horse were several Greek warriors, including Odysseus. Believing that they were safe, King Priam accepted the gift. They brought the horse inside the city, and all of Troy celebrated that the war was over. Only Priam's daughter **Princess Cassandra** warned that it was a trick. She had been born with the gift of **prophecy**, meaning that she could see some parts of the future. However, she had also been cursed by the god **Apollo** so that no one would ever believe her.

After the celebrations were over and the Trojans were sleeping, Odysseus and the Greek warriors crept out of the wooden horse and unlocked the city gates. The Greeks who left in their ships had all returned, and they charged into the city, set it on fire, and easily defeated the surprised Trojans. Paris shot Achilles in his heel with a poison arrow during this last battle, killing the great warrior. This is why the term "**Achilles' heel**" is still used today to describe someone's point of weakness. Both Paris and King Priam were eventually overwhelmed and killed by the invading army, and Princess Cassandra was captured and taken back to Mycenae by King Agamemnon. When King Menelaus found Helen, he raised his sword to kill her, but he couldn't do it. She returned with him to Sparta to again be their queen.

The story of the Trojan War was written by a blind poet named **Homer** in his stories called <u>**The Iliad**</u> and <u>**The Odyssey**</u>, but many other people have told them countless times. Each person who tells it usually ends up telling it a little differently. In fact, if you check the details of the story from this book, you'll find that someone else has told parts of the story another way. That's both the fun of Greek history and a problem for historians: they simply don't know which version is correct. They do think that the war really happened though, and that the kings, queens, heroes, and heroines were real people. Many of the events were exaggerated, and it's unlikely that gods and goddesses were involved, but it's a story that's hard to forget!

Chapter 1: Vocabulary Activity:

Can you match each word, person, or place with the correct description?

1)	City-state	a)	The Mycenaeans' main city-state
2)	Minotaur	b)	A Trojan Princess
3)	Ariadne	c)	A complicated maze
4)	Cassandra	d)	Telling history as stories instead of writing it down
5)	Mycenae	e)	A rival city-state of Mycenaeans
6)	Troy	f)	A city-sized country
7)	Labyrinth	g)	A monster with a human body and a bull's head
8)	Oral History	h)	A Minoan Princess

Almost everyone today has heard about the Olympic Games, but did you know that they began in Ancient Greece in 776 BCE? That's nearly 3,000 years ago! All free Greek-speaking men were eligible to compete in the athletic

https://pixabay.com/es/photos/grecia-olympia-sitio-106227/

competitions. Unfortunately for ancient Greek women, there was no women's Olympics, and they weren't allowed to compete against men. Ancient Greek society also had **slavery**, and **slaves** were forbidden from the competition as well. Slavery is when people are forced to work and don't have the same freedom as other people, and it's something that has existed in a lot of places throughout history. Slavery in Ancient Greece is a topic this book will cover in more detail later and was different from slavery in the early United States in some important ways.

The Ancient Greek version of the Olympic Games would have looked quite different from the Olympic Games that you've seen. For one, all the athletes competed naked! Secondly, they only had individual competitions. There were no team sports like basketball, soccer, or even relay races. Finally, many of their competitions don't exist in the modern Olympic Games. While they had events like running, wrestling, and boxing, they also had some others we'd find strange. Their games were closely related to war, and speed and combat were the most important skills for the athletes. The winning athletes were considered the best warriors in Ancient Greece. Because of this, there was no prize for second or third place. Only the winners of each event were rewarded with a crown of olive leaves called a **wreath**.

Running Events

When you learned that Ancient Greek Olympic athletes competed naked, you probably weren't thinking about their shoes. But that's what made their running events the most different from the modern games: runners had to go barefoot. The first ancient Olympic Games only had one race called the **stadion**. Twenty men at a time lined up for a 700-foot sprint to be named the fastest man in Greece. Later games introduced longer races and combined running with other events.

Pankration

Wrestling and boxing were separate sports in the Ancient Greek Olympics, but they were also combined into a sport called **Pankration**, making it a lot like modern **mixed martial arts**. Competitors would cover themselves in olive oil to make it difficult for their opponent to get a good hold on them, and fights could even go to the death if a losing athlete refused to give up. The only rules were no biting and no gouging your opponent's eyes.

RickyBennison, CC0, via Wikimedia Commons
https://commons.wikimedia.org/wiki/File:Greek_Pankratists_2.jpg

Pentathlon

The **Pentathlon** was a series of five different events. The name comes from the Greek words "pente" which means five (like a _pent_agon has five sides) and "athlon" which means contest. In the Ancient Greek version of the Pentathlon, the sports were running, long jump, discus toss, **javelin** (spear) throw, and wrestling.

Internet Archive Book Images, No restrictions, via Wikimedia Commons
https://commons.wikimedia.org/wiki/File:Greek_athletic_sports_and_festivals_(1910)_(14583572389).jpg

Equestrian

The **Equestrian** competitions were the most thrilling and dangerous of the Ancient Greek Olympic Games. These were the events that involved horses, and the most popular was the **four-horse chariot race**. This race became so dangerous that eventually, the owners of the horses and chariot began to hire other people to drive them, called **charioteers**. Their powerful horses would thunder around a track called the **Hippodrome** twelve times. The whole race was about a mile long, with thousands of spectators screaming their support with each lap. If the charioteers lost control, they would collide with other chariots, crash into the walls, and often get trampled by the horses behind them when they tumbled into the dirt.

Ancient Greece

Olimpia

Ancient Greeks took these games so seriously that any warring city-states would call a temporary **truce**. This allowed athletes and spectators to travel safely to southwest Greece to participate or to watch the games. Even more, the games were named after the home of their most important gods and goddesses, whom they believed to live at the top of **Mt. Olympus**. The mountain is a real place, but not where the games were held. They took place in a place called **Olympia**, named in honor of the games. When the athletes competed, they believed they were proving themselves worthy to their gods and goddesses led by **Zeus**.

This connection to their gods and goddesses led to the end of the Olympics in 393 CE. The Romans had conquered Greece by then, and the Roman leaders had converted to Christianity. Emperor Theodosius banned the games because worshiping more than one God was not allowed under new Roman laws. That was the end of the Olympics until European countries started to hold similar competitions in the 1800s CE. In 1896 CE, these countries united to hold the first modern Olympic Games in Athens, and like the Ancient Greek games, these have been held every four years. Unlike the Greeks, some major world events have disrupted or canceled the modern Olympics. **World War I** led to the cancellation of the 1916 games, **World War II** spoiled the 1940 and 1944 games, and the **COVID-19 pandemic** delayed the 2020 Tokyo games by one year.

CHAPTER 2: COMPREHENSION ACTIVITY: TRUE OR FALSE

Can you figure out which of the following statements about the Olympic Games are true and which are false?

1) The ancient Olympic Games are held every four years.

2) The modern Olympic Games have never been cancelled or delayed.

3) Pankration was a lot like modern mixed martial arts.

4) The Ancient Greeks gave awards to the top five athletes in each event.

5) javelin throwing was part of the Ancient Greek Pentathlon.

6) Equestrian events were help in the Hippodrome.

7) The games took place of the base of Mt. Olympus.

8) The first event created in for Olympics was the Stadion.

After the Mycenaean Period ended, Greece entered a **dark age** from 1100 - 850 BCE. Dark ages are when civilizations start to fall apart, and people struggle with basic things like having enough to eat. They are the opposite of a **golden age**. Usually, there are

no clear leaders, or leaders change too frequently to get anything done. In fact, one of the main reasons historians call them dark ages is because there isn't much known about them. Fewer things are being invented or written down during these times, so they're kind of like gaps in history. Remember, history isn't just what happened; it's the record of what happened. Things that didn't get remembered or recorded can't be learned about anymore. Dark ages are sad because they are hard times and because they are lost to us.

The two most powerful and important Greek city-states that followed the dark age were Athens and Sparta. Ancient Greeks all spoke the same language and had similar beliefs, but each city-state was also a lot like an independent country. Both Athenians and Spartans believed that they were the most "Greek" and the leaders of the Greek world.

Eventually, a thirty-year war was needed to settle the dispute. During what's called the **Archaic Period** that lasted from 800 - 500 BCE, however, the rivalry remained mostly peaceful.

Athens During the Archaic Period (800-500 BCE)

Athens grew and thrived for two main reasons. First, it was located by the sea and had a port for ships. This meant that **merchants** could sail directly to Athens with  things to sell and trade from all around the Mediterranean Sea. This brought a lot of money and people into the city-state. Secondly, it was built around a large hilltop called the **Acropolis** that was easy to defend in times of war. So, Athenians could remain relatively safe, and other groups couldn't take it over. Unlike Sparta, Athens was one of the only Greek city-states that didn't fall to invaders during the dark age.

Because city-states worked a lot like modern countries, they also each had their own leaders. In the Archaic Period, Athens was an **oligarchy**. Instead of having a king, an oligarchy is ruled by a small group of wealthy and powerful citizens called **aristocrats**. This kind of system usually ends up being very good for the rich. They make laws and decisions that help themselves but not the rest of the people. The system is typically unfair to the people who don't have the rights or power to change things.

Archaic Athens had leaders called **archons** who were chosen by the aristocrats. A few of them tried to make some **reforms** or government changes. One named **Draco** decided that it was important to write all their laws down. In 622 BCE, he displayed them publicly in Athens' town square called the **agora**. He was tired of the aristocrats changing them around all the time or making up new ones whenever it helped them. Unfortunately, the laws that Draco wrote down were extremely harsh. He wasn't very creative in his punishments, and most of the penalties were death. This made the system more fair but even less popular, and Draco was **exiled**. To this day, the word **draconian** is used to describe someone or something that is too harsh, severe, or violent.

The aristocrats replaced Draco with **Solon** in 594 BCE. They hoped he would create reforms that would calm the people of Athens after Draco's bloodshed but still let them keep power. One of Solon's reforms

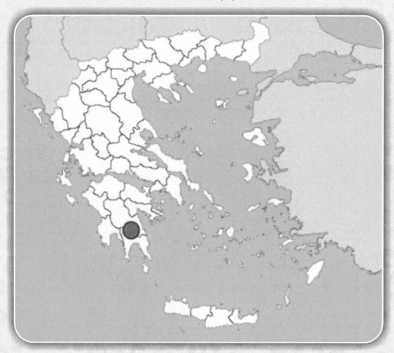

was to start the **Assembly** where Athenian men could come to vote on some important issues. He also began choosing judges with a lottery so that poor Athenians could also be chosen. Lastly, he redistributed land and made certain kinds of slavery illegal - which was the beginning of **democratic** ideas in Athens, where more and more citizens could participate in the government.

Sparta During the Archaic Period (800-500 BCE)

Unlike Athens, the Mycenaean city-state of Sparta fell to a group of invaders called the **Dorians** during the dark age. The culture that developed there is a mixture of Dorian and Spartan. They became a **warrior culture** and continued to win battles, take more slaves, and grow in population. They had two kings - each descended from one of the twins who conquered Sparta after the Trojan War. The people of Sparta were divided into three main groups: citizens, perioikoi (*pair-ee-oh-eye-koy*), and helots (*hel-luts*).

Spartan **citizens** were people who could prove that they were born Spartan. Sometimes this meant paying someone to research their family to show that their parent, grandparents, or great-grandparents didn't come from somewhere else. If you could prove your citizenship, you were given good housing and certain rights, like getting a trial if they were accused of a crime. The other groups weren't promised this, but the **perioikoi** were at least allowed to travel freely, own land, and become traders. Perioikoi means "neighbors" because these were people from the area around the city-state of Sparta that they controlled. The **helots** were the lowest group. They were slaves who had been captured during war and brought into Sparta to farm their land. They could buy more land, but they never technically owned it - and they weren't allowed to leave. Every harvest, they had to give half of the crop to their Spartan masters.

SAWg3rd, CC0, via Wikimedia Commons
https://commons.wikimedia.org/wiki/File:Spartan
_Warrior_Agoge.jpg

To keep their army strong, Spartans began training their boys when they were only seven years old! They would be taken from their homes and raised in a military school called an **agoge** until they were twenty. During this time, they were treated cruelly by their teachers and trainers. They would beat them and leave them out in the cold to try and make them tougher. They would stop feeding them and force them to steal food to survive. If they got caught, they would be whipped as punishment. Those that survived were well-trained soldiers, but many of the boys died before their school was over. The Spartans were so obsessed with being strong for war that they would abandon newborn babies if they were physically deformed or too small. They would be left outside to either die or be found and raised by strangers from the perioikoi or helot classes. Dying in battle was considered an honor for Spartan men. When they left for war, they were told that they needed to return either *with* their shield (victorious) or it (dead). If they tried to come back without their shield, they would be considered a deserter or a coward and be **shunned** by other Spartans.

Because most Spartan men were soldiers, Spartan women did many of the other jobs in the city-state. Women owned land and businesses and were relied upon, especially in times of war, to keep things running. Because of this, women in Sparta were better educated and had more far more freedoms than women in Athens. Women in Athens didn't go to school past the age of twelve, needed men to **escort** them through the city, and weren't allowed to vote when they became a democracy.

As you've seen, slavery was a big part of both Athenian and Spartan life. Slaves in Greece were usually people who were captured when their city or town was taken over in war, but they could also be made slaves as punishment for a crime. Greek slaves sometimes had certain rights, and they didn't always stay a slave for their whole life.

For example, if you owed someone money in Athens but couldn't pay them back, you could be sentenced to slavery. This sentence would last for an agreed amount of time, and then your debt was paid off. In Sparta, helots weren't allowed to leave the land they lived on, but they weren't allowed to be bought and sold, and they were guaranteed to keep half of what they grew. None of this makes slavery okay, but it does make it different from the **racial slavery** (owning dark-skinned people) that developed in the early United States and other places worldwide. In this form of slavery, people were considered property instead of human beings and could be bought and sold. Not only that, their children and grandchildren and every person after would be born into slavery for their whole lives. The only way out was for a master to free them, but that wasn't common. The United States outlawed slavery in 1865 CE - after a bloody civil war - but slavery stayed a part of Greek culture until the very end of that culture.

Did you know that saying something that happened in 850 BCE is the same as saying it happened in 850 BC? BCE means Bfore the Common Era, and BC stands for Before Chirst. These abbreviations are used if things happened before the year zero. If events happened afterwards, we use CE which stands for Common Era, but you may also see AD, which stands for Anno Domini ("Year of our Lord" in Latin). For example, it means the same thing to say that World war II started in 1939 CE or 1939 AD.

The change was made because these dates are used by almost the whole world now, and about 70% of the world in non-christian. It would be very confusion if everyone used calendars for their own religious figures, though. We'd all live in different years and history would be very difficult to study! So, the numbers were kept but the names were changed to be ore inclusive of everyone's culture and beliefs.

On another piece of paper, use a ruler to draw a line 9 inches long. Starting at 1, make marks every inch until your reach 8 inches. Above each mark, write the following dates: 1200 BCE, 1100 BCE, 850 BCE, 800 BCE, 776 BCE, 622 BCE, 594 BCE, and 500 BCE. Using the list the events below, write each one below the timeline at the correct date:

Solon's Reforms, the First Olympic Games, The End of the Archaic Period, The Beginning of the Dark Age, The Beginning of the Trojan War, Draco Writes Athenian Laws, The Beginning of the Archaic Period, The End of the Dark Age.

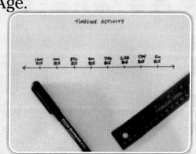

Materials:

- One Sheet of Paper

- One Pen, Pencil, or Marker

- Ruler

For all their adventures, the Greeks' culture and territory stayed limited to the lands in and around the Aegean Sea. All of that changed when **King Cyrus the Great** of **Persia** began taking over their **Ionian** (*eye-own-nee-un*) city-states in modern-day Turkey. Those new territories meant that Persia controlled the huge territory from the Aegean Sea all the way to the Indus River in modern-day Pakistan. The defeated Ionians continued to rebel against the Persians, and other Greek city-states sent them weapons to help them. The Persians decided that to end the **Ionian Revolt,** they would have to conquer all the Greeks.

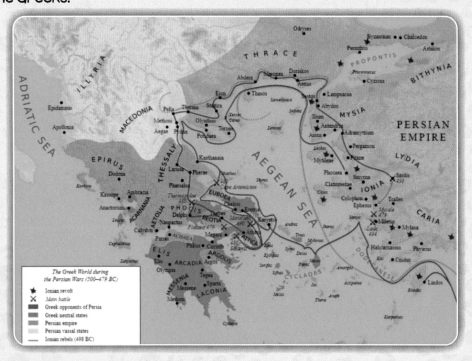

User:Bibi Saint-Pol, CC BY-SA 3.0
<http://creativecommons.org/licenses/by-sa/3.0/>, via Wikimedia
Commons https://commons.wikimedia.org/wiki/File:Map_Greco-Persian_Wars-en.svg

In 490 BCE, the new Persian king (named **Darius I**) sent twenty thousand soldiers to invade the Greek mainland, and they landed near the town of **Marathon** to avoid the feared Athenian navy. They planned to march the army into Athens, but the Athenians quickly gathered an army. About ten thousand Greek soldiers raced to cut off the Persian force, led by **General Miltiades.** The Persians opened fire on them with their

https://commons.wikimedia.
org/wiki/File:Greek-Persian_duel.jpg

longbows, but the Greeks ducked behind their **bronze** shields to form a metallic wall to block the hail of arrows. Miltiades knew that they were outnumbered, and he had to think quickly before they were overwhelmed. He lined up the entire Greek army and ordered a charge at the surprised Persian forces.

Everything happened so fast that the Persians didn't notice there were fewer soldiers in the middle of the Greek line! When the two armies clashed, the Persians in the center quickly defeated their opponents (at first) but then found themselves trapped between the deeper rows of Greeks who had charged on their left and right. They were surrounded, with the well-trained Greek soldiers closing in from both sides. The Persian generals saw the chaos and ordered a retreat to their ships, leaving over 6,000 of their own troops dead - but less than 200 Greeks had died in battle.

Once the Persians reached their ships, they began sailing directly to Athens in a last, desperate chance to save their mission. One of the Greek soldiers, Pheidippides, was ordered to run to Athens before the

Persians could arrive. He needed to tell them that they had won, but the enemy fleet was now coming for them. Most Athenians had been expecting their army to lose. The battle was supposed to buy them time to pack up and leave to avoid death or slavery. They were shocked when Pheidippides arrived to deliver his message - he was panting and out of breath - and then they were devastated when he dropped dead from exhaustion! He had run as fast as he could for 26.2 miles from Marathon to Athens. Today's modern marathon race is named in honor of his heroic effort. The Athenians quickly staffed their ships, and when the Persians saw the navy ready for them, they decided to sail home instead.

Ten years later, Darius' son, **Xerxes** (*zerk-zees*), was king, and he wanted to finish what his father had started. This time they didn't underestimate the Greek army, and in 480 BCE, the Persians sent one thousand warships with two hundred thousand soldiers across the Aegean Sea. Even with such a huge force, they wanted to catch the Greeks off guard. They landed far away from strong city-states like Athens and Sparta.

They chose a part of the Greek coast called **Thermopylae** (*thur-mop-po-lee*), and once again, they planned to march their army into Athens. The Greeks discovered this plan, but it was too late. The Greeks sent away most of their men, leaving only three hundred

Spartans and about a thousand of their allies behind to ensure they could leave safely. King Leonidas I led them.

The Persians, however, didn't realize what a bad spot they'd chosen to land in. Mountains on one side the sea on the other forced them to march towards a narrow mountain pass. The Spartans knew this! Led by King Leonidas I, they arrived in time to block the way. The size of the Persian army was useless in such a tight space. They could only send a small number of their soldiers through at a time, and the three hundred Spartan

Jean Housen,
CC BY-SA 4.0 <https://creativecommons.
org/licenses/by-sa/4.0>, via Wikimedia Commons
https://commons.wikimedia.org/wiki/File:20211113_sparti244.jpg

warriors they met there had been *training their entire lives* for a fight like this one. The Persians sent wave after wave into the pass, and wave after wave was beaten by the Leonidas and the mighty Spartans.

When Xerxes realized that he couldn't overwhelm them with numbers, he sent his elite soldiers called the **Immortals** to lead the next charge. They, too, were defeated and turned back. Finally, the Persians found a hidden path to the top of the cliffs, and they fired arrows into the Spartans below. All three hundred Spartans and most of the other Greeks were killed, including King Leonidas.

The Greeks had done their job, though, and they delayed the Persian army long enough to put together a much larger army. Still, they couldn't save Athens, and the Persian army stormed onwards to capture and destroy the proud city-state. The Greeks made the hard decision of letting them take Athens to stop them from marching deeper in Greek territory. The Persians and Greek forces met again in the naval battle at the **Straits of Salamis**. The Persians had a similar problem to the one they had in Thermopylae as their large ships struggled to maneuver in the cramped waterway. The smaller, quicker Greek ships called **triremes** (*try-reems*) were able to row into them and ram them with their **prow** (*the front part of the ship*), causing them to sink.

After this unexpected loss, Xerxes fled back to Asia, but he left half of his army with General **Mardonius** to try and finish off the Greeks at the **Battle of Plataea** in 479 BCE. As usual, the Greek troops were very outnumbered. Compared to the one hundred thousand Persian soldiers, the Greek city-states combined to create an army of about forty thousand led by **Pausanias** *(paw-sah-nee-us)*, the nephew of Leonidas. They faced off across a river, with neither side wanting to cross it. The Greeks finally charged, and the Persians showered them with arrows. Pausanias ordered a retreat before they reached the river, but the whole thing was a trick to get the Persians to cross over follow them. Once half of their army was across, a Spartan force ambushed them both sides, and the Greeks who retreated earlier now turned back to charge the Persians once again. Meanwhile, an Athenian force had slipped away and attacked the Persians that remained on the other side of the river. The surviving Persians retreated, and the invasion was over.

Afterward, the Greeks formed the **Delian League** in 478 BCE to defend against future invasions and to take back the Ionian city-states still under Persian control. The Greeks even took some Persian territories but returned those to them in 449 BCE when the two sides finally made peace.

CHAPTER 4: CREATIVE ACTIVITY:

Create a Greek myth about the Persian Wars!

The Ancient Greeks loved to mix their history with their mythology. These stories usually had a pattern, so follow the steps below to write your very own Greek myth!

1) Create a hero or heroine and give them a Greek-sounding name.

2) Describe who they are and what made them special.

3) Give your character a mission to accomplish or a problem to solve.

4) Choose one historical figure from Chapter 4 and at least two Greek gods or goddesses from the list below. One will help your character and one will try to stop them.
   - Zeus: God of Thunder and king of the Gods
   - Artemis: Goddess of the Hunt
   - Ares: God of War
   - Apollo: God of Archery
   - Hephaestus: God of Smiths and Metalworking
   - Aphrodite: Goddess of Love
   - Athena: Goddess of Wisdom

5. Use three to five real events from the Greco-Persian Wars as you explain how your hero or heroine succeeded (or failed) in completing their mission or solving their problem!

https://www.pexels.com/photo/the-parthenon-in-greece-5961718/

After Solon made his reforms in 594 BCE, some other aristocrats got the idea that they could manipulate the people of Athens and use their popularity to gain power. An aristocrat named **Peisistratus** convinced the people that he would solve all of their problems, but he only did it to gain control over the other aristocrats. He made the people of Athens loyal to him, and the other aristocrats were afraid to challenge him. This is called **mob rule**, and Peisistratus became the **Tyrant** of Athens from 561 - 527 BCE. A tyrant is someone who rules through popularity and loyalty, but it's very different from democracy. In a democracy, there are laws, and people have rights. In a **tyranny**, the leader can do whatever they want, and popularity isn't carefully measured by votes. If they lose popularity, they are overthrown. This usually happens when they can't keep their promises and a new tyrant takes over. This is what happened in Athens until **Cleisthenes** (cliss-ten-nees) came along in 508 BCE and **Athenian Democracy** was born, kicking off the **Classical Period of Ancient Greece** (500 - 323 BCE).

Cleisthenes saw that tyrants were able to take over because of the loyalty they got from leaders of different **clans** in Athens. These family clans controlled different parts of the city-state, and people mostly followed their clan leaders. To get rid of this old system of loyalty and change it into something more democratic, he sorted everyone in Athens into ten new groups called **tribes** that had nothing to do with family. Each of these ten tribes was a mixture of people from the old clans, and they had to cooperate and work together in their new groups. This made family loyalty less important for politics, made it more difficult for tyrants to get power, and made it easier for each person to make their own decisions.

In 461, a new leader named **Pericles** (*pair-uh-cleez*) increased the importance of the Assembly. Under Cleisthenes, the Assembly voted on some things, but the archons and tyrants made all the big decisions. Pericles changed this so that the Assembly voted on all important decisions, such as going to war and how to spend the city's money. Pericles was a very skilled **orator** and

could usually persuade the Assembly to vote for what he wanted. This ability might be explained by his career as an actor and performer before he got into politics! Pericles also realized that even though all male Athenian citizens could join the Assembly, few were coming. It wasn't because they didn't care or didn't want to, but because it meant taking time away from their jobs. Poor and working Athenians couldn't do this. Aristocrats got their wealth from the land they owned, so they didn't have to go to work like the rest of the people. Pericles made a new law that paid every citizen for their time taking part in the Assembly, and the number of people who came to speak and vote skyrocketed.

Pericles took this idea further and paid people to be judges and work on projects that would beautify Athens. This kept Pericles very popular, and many of the famous ruins and sculptures that can still be found in Athens were made during this time. The most famous of his monuments was a massive temple to the goddess **Athena** called the **Parthenon**. It was built on the Acropolis, and its huge scale and careful artistry was a celebration of Greek culture. It represented their victory against the Persians, who had destroyed the original temple on the famous hilltop. For thirty-two years, the old temple sat untouched and in ruins as a memorial for the war. Pericles decided that it was finally time to rebuild, and it's now one of the most famous buildings in the entire world. Above its giant marble pillars and just below its equally marbly roof was a (you guessed it) marble sculpture called a **frieze** that circled the entire temple. It went for an incredible 524 feet around the perimeter, and its 114 blocks showed scenes of Greek history, culture, and **mythology**.

These changes made life for Athenians more democratic, more beautiful, and more prosperous. Outside of Athens, Pericles was creating an empire through the Delian League. This was the group of over three hundred city-states and territories scattered in and around the Aegean Sea. They formed an **alliance** (they agreed to defend and help each other) in 478 BCE to prevent more attacks by Persia. Some remained **allies** of Athens by the time of Pericles, but some were controlled by Athens more forcefully. Because of this, the Delian League is also sometimes called the Athenian League or the **Athenian Empire**. By being the leader of its allies and controlling the

other territories, Athens grew very wealthy. In fact, this is where Pericles got all the money to pay his citizens for taking part in government and building the Acropolis projects.

The Delian League was meant to unify the Greek city-states, but it eventually started tearing them apart. Sparta remained fiercely independent, and they didn't like it when Athens used the league to start taking territory from some of their allies. The **Golden Age of Athens** began in 479 BCE after the Persian invasion, and it ended in 431 BCE with the outbreak of the Peloponnesian War. Less than sixty years after teaming up to kick the Persians out of Greece, Athens and Sparta started a war with each other.

Chapter 5: Vocabulary Activity:

Can you match each word, person, or place with the correct description?

1) Golden Age of Athens	a) The Temple of Athena on the Acropolis
2) Cleisthenes	b) The leader who got rid of family clans
3) Parthenon	c) A speaker and-or debater
4) Orator	d) The period of Greek history from 500-323 BCE
5) Pericles	e) Groups with family-based loyalty in Athens
6) Clans	f) The leader who paid people to come to the Assembly
7) Tribes	g) The new groups that made Athens more democratic
8) Classical Period	h) The time peace and prosperity from 479-431 BCE

The Peloponnesian War *(pell-oh-puh-neez-shun)* between Athens, Sparta, and their allies lasted from 431 - 404 BCE, with tens of thousands of deaths on each side. The war started because of Athens' rapid rise to power during and after the Persian Wars.

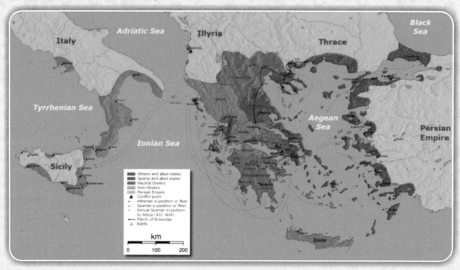

Translator was Kenmayer, CC0, via Wikimedia Commons
https://commons.wikimedia.org/wiki/File:Pelop_war_en.png

Athens was gaining this power through the Delian League. It started as just an oath and a shared bank account. All the members agreed to work together to prevent another Persian invasion, and they all contributed money called a **tribute** and kept it in a **treasury** that would be used to strengthen their armies and navies. The problem was that Athenians controlled the treasury, and the main naval fleet was kept by Athens. After a while, city-states were just paying Athens, and Athens decided how to use the money. One city-state called **Naxos** agreed that they wanted to leave the league, and Athens sent their navy to force them to keep paying tribute. The League had become an empire, and Athens was its capital.

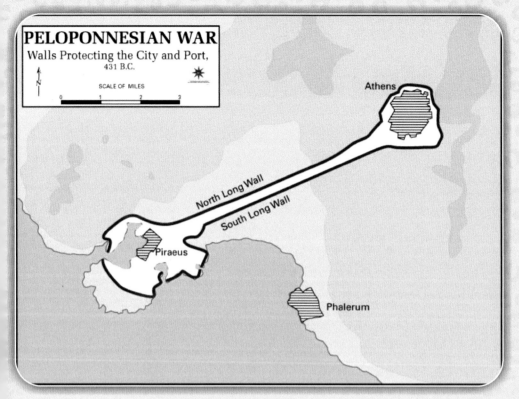

Sparta worried that Athens' power would eventually spread to challenge them, and they wanted to start the fight before Athens got any stronger. They didn't have a navy, so their first move was to invade the land surrounding Athens. Sparta had the strongest army, so Pericles avoided leaving the city and meeting them in the open. Athens had built fortifications called the **Long Walls** around their city and along the four-mile path to the coast at **Piraeus** *(Pie-ree-us),*

where they kept their massive fleet. This kept the Spartans out and made sure that Athens wasn't cut off from the Delian League, who could send them food and supplies

In 430 BCE, a deadly **plague** (a sickness affecting almost everyone) scorched through Athens, killing about half of their population. Pericles died in the outbreak, and Athens had to hire mercenaries from other city-states to continue fighting. The Spartans feared the plague would infect them and retreated until it passed.   Athens needed a new plan. Many of their experienced soldiers and sailors died, and they used new recruits and mercenaries to keep fighting. They used the treasury of the Delian League to pay as many soldiers as they could, and they began fighting the Spartans in the open. They thought that if they sent enough soldiers to fight them, they could wear them down. Spartans had to train their whole lives, and their numbers would take longer to replace. This kind of war is called **attrition** - meaning that the army got

smaller because of dying soldiers. Like so many before them, though, the Athenians had underestimated the Spartan army. Athens couldn't defeat Sparta in open battle, and Sparta couldn't get past the Athenian walls and defenses. In 421 BCE, the two sides signed a **truce** that lasted until 413 BCE.

The war started up again when Athens got involved in a conflict in **Sicily**. They tried to help their ally **Sicilia** against the city-state of **Syracuse**. Syracuse was an ally of Sparta, and they saw this as proof that war with Athens was **inevitable**. By this time, Sparta had trained sailors and built a fleet of their own, and Athens could no longer dominate the seas. Sparta also started to get support from a very unlikely place.

Persia had kept fighting with Athens and the Delian League long after they backed off from Greece, and they saw them as the bigger problem. They followed the saying, **"the enemy of my enemy is my friend,"** and began sending money and supplies to Sparta. By 404 BCE, Athens was once again surrounded by its enemies. They had lost almost their entire naval fleet to the Spartan general **Lysander** in the **Battle of Aegospotami**, and their people were now on the edge of starvation inside their city. Athens was forced to surrender, burn what was left of their fleet, give up their territories, and tear down their walls. They were now part of Sparta's new empire.

Can you figure out which of the following statements about the Peloponnesian War are true and which are false?

1) Athens attacked Sparta in 431 BCE because they were becoming too powerful.

2) Athens used the Delian League to create wealth and power for themselves.

3) The Spartans allied with Persia during the second part of the war.

4) Sparta lost about half of its population to a plague in 430 BCE.

5) Pericles was a aggressive and tried to fight the Spartans in open combat.

6) The Spartans began the war with a better navy than Athens.

7) There was constant fighting from 431-404 BCE.

8) Sparta defeated Athens in 404 BCE and forced them to take down their long walls.

As Athens and Sparta were wearing themselves out in the south of Greece, a new power was growing in the north. A city-state called **Pella** had gained control of the whole region of **Macedonia** and wanted more. Under the leadership of **King Philip II**, they had reformed their army and made improvements to traditional Greek weapons, armor, and fighting style.

https://commons.wikimedia.org/wiki/File:
Philip_II_of_Macedon_CdM.jpg

Greek soldiers, called **hoplites**, always carried a circular shield, a spear, and a short sword for close fighting. Helmets, breastplates, and other body armor were common, but each hoplite had to buy their own armor. The poor peasants who fought usually didn't have these. The hoplites would move in **phalanx** *(flay-lanks)* formation, which meant standing shoulder to shoulder with the people next to them, with at least seven soldiers standing behind the front line. When someone on the front line was wounded, the next person was ready to step up and take their place. Each hoplite's shield overlapped with the shields next to them, making the entire phalanx like an armored shell. The hoplites' spears kept the enemy from getting too close, and archers' arrows usually couldn't pierce their shields made of wood, leather, and copper.

Philip grew the size of the Macedonian army from ten thousand volunteer soldiers to twenty-four thousand professional soldiers. They were given uniforms, weapons, and armor and swore an oath to be loyal to their king. Other Greek soldiers fought for the city-state, but the Macedonian army fought for their king no matter where they were from, so Philip could recruit soldiers from all over his growing empire.

The shields his soldiers carried were smaller and lighter, allowing them to be quicker than other Greek armies. He also changed to spears called **sarissas** *(sar-riss-iss)* that were almost triple the length of traditional hoplite spears. This let the first three rows of the phalanx hold their spears forward into a charging enemy. These changes were successful for Philip as he took more and more territory in Greece. In 338 BCE, he won the **Battle of Chaeronea** *(karen-nee-uh)* against Thebes and Athens. He took control of Athens' rebuilt navy, and he created the League of Corinth with himself as the leader, making him the leader of all the

Greek city-states except for Sparta, who refused to join. Philip let this go and instead looked east with plans to invade the Persian Empire. In 336 BCE, he was assassinated by one of his bodyguards, and his invasion plans were left to his son, Alexander.

Alexander III, or better known as Alexander the Great, became King of Macedonia at the age of twenty. He had helped his father in many battles as a teenager, but invading Persia was a very different story. The Greeks had spent over a hundred years defending against the Persian Empire, but to try and invade them seemed like madness. But Alexander was a great **strategist** -as well as a great warrior; this means he figured out the best ways to win battles. He knew Greek history and realized that he would need to keep putting down rebellions if he stayed in Greece. By carrying out his father's plans to invade Persia, Alexander united the Greek city-states against their ancient enemy. In 334 BCE, Alexander took fifty thousand Macedonian and other Greek soldiers across the sea to battle the 200,000-strong army of mighty Persia.

The first big fight was the Battle of Granicus, and it took place near the site of Ancient Troy. Alexander and his army used their phalanx formation and sarissas to win a hard victory and marched deeper into Persian territory. As they went, Alexander paid his soldiers by allowing them to **plunder** the cities that surrendered to him. This meant that they were only paid if they were successful, and it also encouraged them to keep going to earn more money and valuable items. Many Greeks lived in this part of Persia - called Asia Minor - and Alexander

recruited and trained more soldiers to replace those he lost. Others were recruited to help them carry their food, weapons, and other supplies on their long journey to the heart of the Persian Empire.

The next big fight for Alexander and his army was the **Battle of Issus** in 333 BCE. This time the Persian **King Darius III** himself showed up to lead his army, but Alexander was victorious again. Darius was forced to flee, marking the first time that an army led by the Persian king was defeated. Deeper into the vast Persian Empire, Alexander and his army fought, winning each battle and claiming new land as his own. He met King Darius again at the **Battle of Gaugamela** *(gog-ug-mee-luh)*, where he sent his fearsome war chariots in a charge at the center of Alexander's phalanx. The Macedonian phalanx quickly split apart, creating a gap for the chariots to run through harmlessly. They turned

around to make another run at Alexander's army, but the Macedonians were ready to take advantage of their slowdown, attacking them from both sides. The phalanx then came back together and charged the Persian line, which broke and scattered. Darius fled once again, and Alexander's army had its most important victory yet.

They pursued Darius, plundering **Babylon** and **Susa** as they went. When they caught up to the Persian king in **Bactria**, he was already dead. Many Persian aristocrats understood that the war was over, and they began changing sides. It was one of Darius' own relatives named **Bessus** that had captured and killed him. Alexander ordered a grand funeral for Darius, and then continued to the capital of **Persepolis** (pur-sep-po-liss). As a final act of revenge against Persia for their invasion and destruction of Athens, Alexander's army burned the beautiful city to the ground.

Alexander continued to fight all the way to the **Ganges River** in Pakistan and India, where his army defeated a cavalry of war elephants before finally turning back to Babylon to plan his next conquest in **Arabia**. At the age of 32, he had led his army into fifteen battles. Spears had wounded him in his head and chest, and he had been shot with arrows through a leg and one of his lungs. In 323 BCE, he caught a sudden fever, lost his ability to speak, and died. One of the largest empires the world had ever seen was without a leader.

On another piece of paper, use a ruler to draw a line 9 inches long. Starting at 1, make marks every inch until your reach 8 inches. Above each mark, write the following dates: 404 BCE, 338 BCE, 334 BCE, 333 BCE, 331 BCE, 330 BCE and 323 BCE. using the list of events below, write each one below the timeline at the correct date:

> Battle of Gaugamela, The Burning of Persepolis, The Battle of Issus, The Death of Philip II of Macedonia, Battle of Chaeronea, End of the Peloponnesian War, The Death of Alexander the Great, The Beginning of the Persian of Invasion.

Materials:
- One Sheet of Paper
- One Pen, Pencil, or Marker
- Ruler

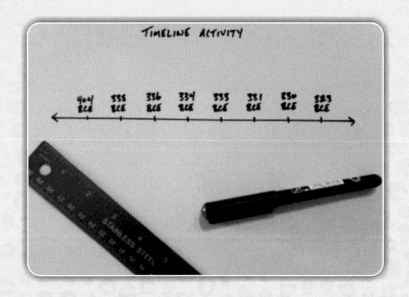

"To the strongest," were the last words that Alexander said before he died. His voice was failing him, and other Macedonian leaders wanted to know who would be the next king of his huge empire. They never got a clear answer, and four of his generals fought each other for years before splitting the territory between them. **Lysimachus** *(lie-she-make-us)* took Thrace and Asia Minor, **Seleucus** *(sel-luke-us)* took the old Persian territory, **Cassander** took Macedonia and Greece, and **Ptolemy** *(tole-lem-mee)* took Egypt, Palestine, and Cyprus. Ptolemy's dynasty ruled as the Pharaohs of Egypt until the death of Cleopatra during Roman times.

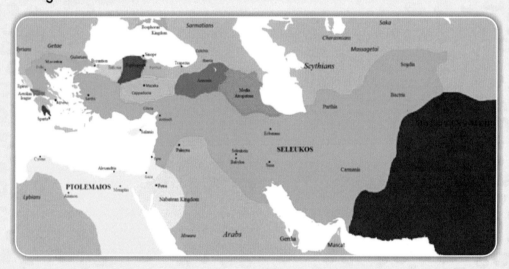

Javierfv1212, CC BY-SA 3.0
<https://creativecommons.org/licenses/by-sa/3.0>,
via Wikimedia Commons https://commons.wikimedia.org/wiki/File:Hellenistic_world_281_B.C..png

All these areas were **Hellenized**, meaning they became more Greek. From 323 BCE until 31 BCE, the period is called the **Hellenistic Age** because of how much Greek culture came to dominate the world. Until Alexander, the Greeks stayed mostly around the Aegean Sea, but their art and ideas were now found everywhere. Temples to Greek

47

PHAROS

goddesses like the **Artemis Temple in Ephesus**, Turkey, and Greek-style buildings like the **Lighthouse of Alexandria**, Egypt, were built across Asia and northern Africa

Speaking of Alexandria, the Macedonian conqueror named dozens of cities across his empire "Alexandria" in his own honor! He even named one after his horse, Bucephalus! Having so many cities with the same name was probably confusing, but the Greek language probably helped people ask for directions. It had become a common tongue that most people through Alexander's old empire could speak or read. This allowed for ideas and stories to spread thousands of miles from where they started. And speaking of thousands of miles, Alexander built many roads that made it easier to trade from Europe all the way to India. This exchange of ideas, goods, and culture made the ancient world start to seem a little bit smaller.

Makeandtoss, CC0, via Wikimedia Commons
https://commons.wikimedia.org/wiki/File:View_of_Qasr_Al-Abd,_Amman.jpg

Back in Greece, people were producing some of the most beautiful art ever created. Their marble sculptures were incredibly realistic and full of emotion and action. That's not easy to do with something that doesn't move! They gave them intense facial expressions and showed them with strained muscles and twisted torsos. This was very different from earlier sculptures that showed people standing still with blank stares. Greek culture was also being influenced by their encounters with so many different people. As they learned about other people's history and religion, the Greeks wrote it down and blended it into their own stories. Because of this, many historians consider the Hellenistic Age a **fusion** of cultures instead of just the spread of Greek culture.

Can you figure out which of the following statements about the Peloponnesian War are true and which are false?

Number 1:

- The Hellenistic Age began in 500 BCE
- Alexander named a city after his horse
- Hellenistic art was full of movement and emotion

Number 2:

- Most of the Hellenistic world spoke or read Greek
- Alexander built roads that made travel and trade easier
- Alexander named Ptolemy as the next king before he died

Number 3:

- The Hellenistic Ages was a fusion of Greek, Asian and African cultures
- Alexander's empire was divided into two parts after he died
- The lighthouse of Alexandria was built in Egypt

The Hellenistic Age marked the end of independent Greek territory until modern times. A new power had developed in the western Mediterranean Sea with its capital in **Rome**. Between 200 and 146 BCE, the Romans began expanding into Spain, North Africa, and Greece.

Pasztilla aka Attila Terbócs, Marsyas, WillyboyDerivative
work: Amphipolis, CC BY-SA 4.0
<https://creativecommons.org/licenses/by-sa/4.0>, via Wikimedia
Commons https://commons.wikimedia.org/wiki/File:Second_Roman%E2%80%93Macedonian_War-en.svg

Rome's rise to power was very similar to Greece's in a lot of ways. Like the Spartans and Macedonians, they were fierce warriors who could conquer the Italian peninsula through their superior training and battle strategies. Like Athens, they developed a democratic form of government where commoners called **Plebeians** *(plee-bee-uns)* had voting rights and political power. They had to take this from the aristocrats called **Patricians** *(puh-trish-uns)*. It wasn't easy, and it took a long time, just like the Athenians' struggle against their oligarchy. The Romans voted for people to represent them in government, so their type of democracy was called a **representative democracy**. Athenians voted directly on issues by joining the Assembly, so their kind of democracy was called a **direct democracy**.

The Romans even share a lot of their myths and stories with the Greeks. In one story called the **Aenid** *(in-nid)*, a group of Trojans led by **Aeneas** *(inn-nee-us)* escaped the burning of their city by the Mycenaean Greeks. They went on a long and difficult journey, with the gods and goddesses helping or harming them until they finally reached Italy. According to the legend, Aeneas was the ancestor of the first king of Rome named **Romulus**.

Rome's first main rival was the city of **Carthage** - in modern-day Tunisia - which is north Africa. The two cities faced each other across the Mediterranean, and eventually, they fought a series of wars called the **Punic Wars**. By the year 200 BCE, Rome had mostly defeated Carthage, and they turned their attention to Macedonia and Greece. As usual, none of the city-states were getting along. The Romans took advantage of this through an alliance with the **Achaean** (eh-kee-un) **League**.

These were the city-states in southern Greece and included many of the usual suspects like Sparta and Corinth. They never accepted or liked the Macedonian rulers, and they joined the Romans against them in the **Second Macedonian War** that lasted from 200 - 197 BCE. After three years of fighting, the Roman **legions** lined up against the feared Macedonian phalanx at the **Battle of Cynoscephalae** (sin-oh-sef-oh-lie). The two evenly matched forces clashed in the rain, mud, and fog until the Romans surrounded the Macedonian soldiers. They raised their sarissas to show their surrender, but the Romans either didn't understand this signal or ignored it. They kept closing in on the Macedonians and slaughtered them. There was chaos, and those who could escape ran away. The Macedonians and Romans met again in Third Macedonian War, and this time the Romans broke their power for good at the Battle of Pydna in 168 BCE.

The Roman legions fought a lot like the Macedonians, but they made some changes to the classic phalanx. Instead of staying in one large block, the Romans lined up more like a chessboard, with blocks of soldiers in a formation that looks a little bit like the dots on the "five" side of playing dice. They also changed their shields, using a taller oval shield that protected their whole body instead of the circular shield of the Macedonians and Greeks.

The Achaean League rejoiced when the Macedonians were finally defeated, but their celebration didn't last long. The Romans no longer needed them as an ally and began to see them as a threat. They ordered the league to **disband**, but they refused and declared war on the much more powerful Romans. The Achaeans were nowhere near as prepared as Macedonia, and the Romans ended the very short war in 146 BCE with the **Battle of Corinth**. The Greeks, defiant until the end, were finally defeated. Still, their culture lived on through the Romans. They plundered Corinth, taking Greek art with them back to Italy that they would later imitate. They were also impressed with their buildings and architecture, and Greek designs inspired many future Roman cities.

Chapter 9: Vocabulary Activity:

Can you match each word, person, or place with the correct description?

1) Disband	a) The Roman's main rival in modern-day Tunisia
2) Battle of Cynoscephalae	b) The battle ended the Roman wars against the Greeks
3) Carthage	c) A Trojan who escaped and fled to Italy
4) Battle of Corinth	d) The fight between Rome and Carthage
5) Aeneas	e) To break apart or end an alliance
6) Punic War	f) The first king of Rome
7) Romulus	g) The Greek city-states that disliked the Macedonians
8) Achaean League	h) An Important Roman victory against Macedonia

The Greeks inspired more than just the Romans. Their civilization began and ended more than two thousand years ago, and modern society is still learning from them. Let's look at a few of the most important Greek leaders, thinkers, and artists to see how their accomplishments still influence us today.

Herodotus

Because this is a history book, **Herodotus** *(hair-ruh-doe-dus)* is at the top of this list. His collection called *Histories* is famous for its accounts of the Greco-Persian wars and other events from the Classical Age. His writings are why the modern world knows so much about the heroics of the three hundred Spartans at Thermopylae and even the events of the Olympic Games. Like most historians

Metropolitan Museum of Art, CC0, via Wikimedia Commons https://commons.wikimedia.org/wiki/File: Cropped-removebg-herodotus-historian.png

today, Herodotus was not a witness to the events he wrote about. He is considered the "**Father of History**" because of his careful interviews and research into important events. If some of the stories seem a little exaggerated, it's only because that's how they were told to him.

Pericles

Pericles *(pair-uh-cleez)* was the most important leader of Athens and was largely responsible for their golden age. He didn't start democracy

https://commons.wikimedia.org/wiki/
File:Pericles_Pio-Clementino_
Inv269_n3.jpg

in Greece, but he kept it moving forward. He saw that giving people the right to vote wasn't enough and that he also needed to give them the ability to vote. This meant paying poor Athenians for their time in the Assembly to make up for what they lost by not working. Pericles still didn't give these rights to Athenian women, and slavery remained a part of Athens until the end. Modern democracies are still working to give everyone the same rights, and like Pericles, they still have a lot of work to do.

Plato and Aristotle

One of the most important thinkers in Ancient Greece was a philosopher named **Plato** (*play-toe*). He wrote an essay called the Republic that tried to figure out all the government problems and even gave a suggestion for a perfect government. Unfortunately, his solution was to have a wise and powerful king, and those were hard to come by. He also wrote about his

https://commons.wikimedia.org/
wiki/File:Sanzio_01_Plato_Aristotle.jpg

teacher named **Socrates** (*sock-ruh-teez*), who may or may not have been a real person. Socrates walked around Athens to talk to people who claimed to be experts. He asked them a bunch of questions until they had to admit that they really didn't know what they were talking about. Socrates' most famous statement is that he was the smartest person alive for the simple reason that he knew that he knew nothing.

Plato started a school in Athens called **The Academy**, and the most famous student to come out of it was **Aristotle** *(air-ris-stot-tul)*. His writings on ethics were influential for thousands of years. His basic philosophy was people should be **virtuous**, which meant developing their good traits and keeping them in balance so that they didn't become bad traits, called **vices**. For example, he called **ambition** a virtue because it helped people to succeed in life. Too little ambition and a person became lazy, and too much ambition could make a person greedy and cruel. Laziness, greed, and cruelty were vices because they represented ambition out of balance. Aristotle was also a **naturalist**, and he tried to **classify** all plants and animals into similar groups. This might sound like just a weird hobby, but it has led to our current understanding of how

https://commons.wikimedia.org/wiki/File:School_of_Athens_Raphael_detail_01.jpg

organisms are related to one another and why we call some things "mushrooms" and other things "reptiles." Aristotle was also a tutor of Alexander the Great before he began his invasion of Persia.

The Mathematicians: Euclid and Archimedes

Euclid *(yuke-lid)* was born in 325 BCE, around the time that Alexander the Great was battling war elephants in India. He is called the **"Father of Geometry"** because he gathered all the ideas around at the time and linked them together. His book called *Elements* started with just five assumptions about geometry called **axioms**. These axioms couldn't be proven but were things that seemed obvious. Using these axioms, he built the entire field of geometry that is still studied today.

https://commons.wikimedia.org/wiki/
File:Domenico-Fetti_Archimedes_1620.jpg

Archimedes *(ar-kuh-meed-deez)* is one of the most brilliant people to have ever lived. He was a mathematician, inventor, engineer, and astronomer who proved many geometric formulas. He also more or less created the field of physics by taking his mathematical theories and applying them to the real world to create **simple machines**. The most famous story about Archimedes is how he figured out how to measure the **volume** of any object (how much space it took up). He was frustrated and unable to come up with an answer, so he decided to take a bath. He filled the tub with just a little too much water, and as he got in, he watched it rise and spill over the edge. "EUREKA!" he shouted in triumph. He realized that the volume of any object would be equal to the volume of water it displaced (how much room it took up), just like his own body pushed the water out of the bathtub.

Sophocles

The Greeks are probably most famous for their incredible stories, and one way they told them was through plays. **Sophocles** (*soff-uh-cleez*) was a **playwright** who lived during the Golden Age of Athens and is most remembered for his story called *Oedipus Rex (Oh-ed-di-puss Rex)*. In this **tragedy**, a king is given a **prophecy** that his infant son will grow up to murder him and marry his wife. The king became afraid and ordered a servant to take the baby to a nearby mountain and kill him. When he got there, he couldn't do it. Instead of killing him, he gave him to a shepherd. He returned to the king and lied, saying that the deed was done. The shepherd raised Oedipus as his own and never told him that he and his wife weren't his birth parents. One day after Oedipus had grown up, he visited an **oracle** that told him the same prophecy that the king received: he would kill his father and marry his mother.

Oedipus was horrified and quickly left town so that the prophecy had no chance of coming true. On his way to **Thebes**, he met an older man on the road, and they got into an argument. The old man hit Oedipus, and Oedipus grabbed him and threw him from his chariot. The fall killed the old man, who was Oedipus' father. He didn't know that yet and continued to Thebes. When he arrived, he met a woman named Jocasta, and they fell in love. Jocasta, you might have guessed, was his mother. Yuck. When they discovered the truth, Jocasta hanged herself, and Oedipus stabbed himself in both of his eyes. The big question that Sophocles wanted the audience to think about was this: **How much control do you have over your own life?** It's a big question and the reason why the play is still read by high school and college students today.

CHAPTER 10: DIG DEEPER!

Choose out of the famous Greeks discussed in this chapter and do some more research. Try to find out the following information:

1) When they were born

2) How old they were when they died

3) An accomplishment that wasn't mentioned in this book

4) Three fun facts

Bonus: Find a picture of them and try to make a costume for yourself from what you can find around the house!

References

Admin. "The Ancient History of the Olympics." Kids Blog, 22 Aug. 1970, www.wcl.govt.nz/blogs/kids/index.php/2016/08/22/the-ancient-history-of-the-olympics/.

"Alexander the Great - History Facts for Kids." History for Kids, 7 Feb. 2020, www.historyforkids.net/alexander.html.

Ancient Greece for Kids - Athens, www.primaryhomeworkhelp.co.uk/greece/athens.htm.

"Ancient Greece for Kids | Learn All Ancient Greek History with This Fun Overview." YouTube, YouTube, 12 Nov. 2019, www.youtube.com/watch?v=RchSJSJAbc0.

"Ancient Greece." Ducksters, www.ducksters.com/history/ancient_greece/decline_and_fall_of_ancient_greece.php.

"Ancient Greece." Ducksters, www.ducksters.com/history/ancient_greece/peloponnesian_war.php.

"Ancient Greece." Ducksters, www.ducksters.com/history/ancient_greece/persian_wars.php.

"Ancient Greece." Ducksters, www.ducksters.com/history/ancient_greek_athens.php.

"Ancient Greece." Ducksters, www.ducksters.com/history/ancient_greek_olympics.php.

"Ancient Greek Olympics - Facts for Kids." History for Kids, 7 Feb. 2020, www.historyforkids.net/ancient-greek-olympics.html.

"Ancient Greek Science Facts for Kids." History for Kids, 7 Feb. 2020, www.historyforkids.net/ancient-greek-science.html.

Cartwright, Mark. "Battle of Thermopylae." World History Encyclopedia, World History Encyclopedia, 4 Sept. 2021, www.worldhistory.org/thermopylae/.

"The City of Athens." History for Kids, 7 Feb. 2020, www.historyforkids.net/the-city-of-athens.html.

"Decline and Fall of Greece." History for Kids, 7 Feb. 2020,
www.historyforkids.net/decline-and-fall-of-greece.html.

"Decline and Fall of Greece." History for Kids, 7 Feb. 2020,
www.historyforkids.net/decline-and-fall-of-greece.html.

Encyclopædia Britannica, Encyclopædia Britannica, Inc.,
kids.britannica.com/kids/article/Peloponnesian-War/390830.

"The Golden Age of Athens." History for Kids For Kids, Nile River, Gods, Maps
and Pyramids, www.history4kids.co/2013/08/the-golden-age-of-athens.html.

"Greco–Persian Wars Facts for Kids." Wikt:Revenge,
kids.kiddle.co/Greco%E2%80%93Persian_wars.

"Greek Philosophers." History for Kids, 7 Feb. 2020,
www.historyforkids.net/ancient-greek-philosophers.html.

"Hellenistic Greece for Kids." Hellenistic Greece for Kids and Teachers -
Ancient Greece

for Kids, greece.mrdonn.org/hellenistic-
greece.html#:~:text=Hellenistic%20means%20imitating%20the%20Greeks,th
e%20people%20around%20the%20Mediterranean.

"Hellenistic Period Facts for Kids." Hellenistic Period Facts for Kids,
kids.kiddle.co/Hellenistic_period.

IkenEdu. "The Golden Age of Ancient Greece." YouTube, YouTube, 3 Dec.
2012,
www.youtube.com/watch?v=Jr4faJfqyG0.

"The Internet Classics Archive: Oedipus the King by Sophocles." The Internet
Classics Archive | Oedipus the King by Sophocles,
classics.mit.edu/Sophocles/oedipus.html.

The Macedonian Conquest of Persia,
sites.psu.edu/alexanderthegreatconquests/the-conquest-of-the-persian-
empire/.

Mark, Joshua J. "Alexander the Great & the Burning of Persepolis." World
History Encyclopedia, World History Encyclopedia, 6 Sept. 2021,
www.worldhistory.org/article/214/alexander-the-great--the-burning-of-
persepolis/#:~:text=After%20Darius%20III's%20defeat%2C%20Alexander,aud

ience%20halls%20which%20had%20made.

"Mycenae Facts for Kids." Mycenae Facts for Kids,
kids.kiddle.co/Mycenae#:~:text=It%20is%20about%2090%20km,BC%20is%2
0called%20Mycenaean%20Greece., www.history4kids.co/2013/08/early-
people-of-greece-and-mycenaeans.html,
kids.britannica.com/kids/article/Trojan-War/353873.

"Olympic Games Facts for Kids." Olympic Games Facts for Kids,
kids.kiddle.co/Olympic_Games#Ancient_Olympics.

"Peloponnesian War Facts for Kids." Peloponnesian War Facts for Kids,
kids.kiddle.co/Peloponnesian_War.

"Peloponnesian War." History for Kids, 7 Feb. 2020,
www.historyforkids.net/peloponnesian-war.html.

The Peloponnesian Wars,
www.penfield.edu/webpages/jgiotto/onlinetextbook.cfm?subpage=1649849.

"Persian Wars Facts for Kids." History for Kids, 17 July 2019,
 www.historyforkids.net/persian-wars.html.

"Philip II of MACEDON Facts for Kids." Philip II of Macedon Facts for Kids,
kids.kiddle.co/Philip_II_of_Macedon.

"Philip II of MACEDON Facts for Kids." Philip II of Macedon Facts for Kids,
kids.kiddle.co/Philip_II_of_Macedon.

Sparta - Ancient Greece for Kids,
www.primaryhomeworkhelp.co.uk/greece/sparta.htm.

"Sparta Facts for Kids." History for Kids, 7 Feb. 2020,
www.historyforkids.net/sparta.html.

Wasson, Donald L. "Battle of Gaugamela." World History Encyclopedia, World
History Encyclopedia, 6 Sept. 2021,
www.worldhistory.org/Battle_of_Gaugamela/.